Sowing S[...]s

By Reginald Perryman

Copyright © 2021 Reginald Perryman

All rights reserved

No part of this book may be reproduced in any manner whatsoever in any form without written permission of the publisher except for brief quotations embodied in critical reviews and articles.

ISBN: 9781734918021

Sowing Seeds for Listing Leads

Introduction

Chapter 1 List and Live

Chapter 2 Hunting and Fishing

Chapter 3 The ACTION items

Chapter 4 The Birds and the Seeds

Chapter 5 The Tools and Skills

Chapter 6 Is it the Seed or the Soil

Chapter 7 Harvest your crops

Chapter 8 Buy More Land

Chapter 9 Hire More Farmers

Chapter 10 Planting

Introduction

Most businesses fail within the first 5 - 7 years. Whether you know it or not, once you become a licensed Real Estate agent, you have just started your own business. This is more about having business in your pipeline 3 - 5 years from now, based on the efforts you are making now.

Imagine you are a mind reader and it's 2020. You walk into a neighborhood, and as you walk by each home, you think about Mr. Simpson at 123 Main will be selling summer 2021, Mr. and Mrs. Johnson will be selling in spring 2021. Ms. Adams will be selling in the winter 2022. Mr. Thompson will be selling in the summer 2020 when his son graduates. Every time you walk into a neighborhood, you go into your mental rolodex.

Regardless of where you are at in your career, you need to be planting seeds for several years in advance.

As a licensed agent, you immediately join the pros the day you receive your license. So you must plan to be ready to compete with the best in your market the day you start. As an experienced agent you have new competition entering your market every day! So you must be ready to compete with new ideas, new energy and the new strategies that the next generation of agents will bring.

The title may imply that this book is about farming, it's not, although we will discuss farming a neighborhood. This book is more about building your listing business pipeline for years to come. At some point in the future you may stop prospecting for new business and your database can still provide you with new and repeat business.

The effort to build and plant the seeds for your business is one thing, but still being around when the harvest comes is another. I see it all the time, new agents get in the business and get some momentum, but not enough immediate business to earn a satisfactory income, and then the next year they get out of the business. What happens next? Well, all the efforts of prospecting start to payoff but they are no longer on the farm. I see agents leave the business and then 3 months later get three leads that they have to refer to another agent who is still licensed, only to get another 2-3 calls the following month. Next thing you know they referred $60,000 worth of commissions in a 4-5 month period. This is a result of sowing seeds and then moving off the farm.

In all honesty some agents did not have the right seeds, soil, and instructions to plant for a fruitful harvest. This means they did not have the right tools, environment, coaching, training or mentorship. But most importantly they may not have the right positive attitude or give the correct effort.

As a real estate agent, broker or office, not having listings is like having a shoe store with no shoes. Imagine if you went to a shoe store and the salesperson said they have to go to another company's shoe store on the other side of town to see what they had in stock. If it wasn't for MLS cooperation, we would probably see less real estate offices and more agents per office. It would not make sense for an agent to belong to an office that did not have enough listing inventory to sell. The MLS cooperation of Realtors in some ways made it easier for agents who do not focus on listing inventory to succeed in our industry.

Websites, like Zillow and Realtor.com, understand that leveraging listing inventory is a way to generate income for their site and attract buyers. Just imagine if these two sites did not have permission to advertise Realtor listings. What would happen? Could they just simply advertise for buyers and sell those leads back to Realtors? Probably not.

One month I was reviewing my advertising and marketing budget. Looking at things like my ROI, number of leads and leads converted to sales, I noticed something very interesting. I noticed in one zip code I was paying for had only <u>23 active listings at the time</u>. This had been the average number of active listings over the past three months. There were 8 other agents paying for leads in the zip code. Of the 9 total agents I was number 4. In order to be number 1 in market share for buyer leads I would have to pay over $1200 in this zip code which was over $900 more than what I was currently paying.

The problem is the new cost did not triple the amount of buyer leads I would receive. Even if I received more leads I would still be competing with the other 8 agents who are receiving leads in the zip code. So I estimated of the 9 agents combined we were receiving just over 100 leads per month in the zip code. With 100 potential buyers and only 23 homes listed, this means that we are paying for 67 additional buyers that we have to sell them a home in another zip code or continue to wait until new listings hit the market in this zip code.

If the buyers consider another zip code, this could also be a challenge because of the amount of available listings. But guess what? The next month will generate 100 more buyer leads and if the average number of listings remains at approximately 23. This means we just paid for 63 more buyers in addition to the current buyers. And not only are the buyer leads adding up but this is just one of the many lead sources selling leads in this area. That's when I realized that I should be spending my money and efforts on seller leads. Even in a buyers market, it is still a better business practice to focus on seller leads. Why? Because you only need one buyer for a listing. It is easier and less expensive to obtain a buyer lead than it is to obtain one listing. If you have a listing in any market, buyers will call.

Why sow seeds for listing leads? The average new agent is thinking about what they can list and sell NOW. The experienced agent is paying for leads, nurturing past clients and more. Every agent should have the goal of adding 1 - 2 sellers in his/her database every day. This means anyone considering selling now, 1 year from now, 5 years from now or when their kids graduate college. The truth is by the time a seller is ready to put their home on the market they already have an agent in mind, will use the agent helping them with their new home purchase, or they will select an agent referred to them by a friend or family member. A small number of these sellers will use their previous realtor because the average Realtor will close and forget them. At best, the top agents will send holiday cards. The elite agents make up the rest who actually stay in contact with past clients 12 - 30 times a year or more.

Only about 10% of potential sellers are Hot Sellers. Depending on your market 1 - 2% of those may be FSBOs. 30 - 40% of them may be Warm Sellers. For example:

- There are 100 potential sellers
- 9 Hot sellers listing with an agent
- 1 FSBO
- 40 Warm Sellers.

You better be top of mind when these 40 Warm Sellers become hot. If not, they will search Google or Zillow for agents in their area.

You have three types of sellers.
1. **Hot Sellers** - These are people who need to sell now. Most likely they have already searched for agents or asked family and friends for referrals. Some of them will list their home For Sale By Owner
2. **Warm Sellers** - These are people who *want* to sell sometime in the near future. They do not need to sell anytime soon. They will become *hot* sellers in 9 - 12 months.
3. **JBS (Just Because Sellers)** - These are prospects that have no real reason or motivation for selling. They may be testing the market. They are likely to list and then not allow showings. They are also likely to list and withdraw the listing within the first 2 - 3 weeks. Some agents will say that these sellers are just BS.

Sowing Seeds for Listing Leads

You want to work with hot and warm sellers at all times. Avoid the JBS. The best part about warm sellers is that they underestimate the time it takes to sell a home. They may say something like I am looking to sell in a year. They actually mean they want to be out of the home within 12 months. You have to probe for more details. If you are in a market and the average days on the market is 90 days plus the time it takes to close, your job is to help them understand the timeline to list and sell a home in your market. This explanation will help them decide to list sooner than they originally estimated

Think like a farmer planting seeds and nurturing those seeds and expecting a crop at a specific time each year. After several years, the farmer can predict approximately what his crops will look like based on the seeds planted. But wait, what happens in a drought or other natural causes? The farmer can adjust. Even when conditions change, a farmer can apply the same methods elsewhere and get a return. Although this return may vary depending on conditions, the farmer can easily adjust once they understand the new land, weather conditions, etc. Even if he decides to stay on the same land he can adjust to the new environment.

If you ever go to a conference or training you can always hear an experienced agent say "I wish I would have done this years ago" or "I wish I knew this 5 - 10 years ago". The reason they say this is because they could have planted seeds years ago that would have led to great returns now.

Chapter 1
List and Live

If I learned anything in Real Estate is that you have to be able to switch from Listing Agent to Investor in a matter of seconds during your listing appointment. Should I list this home or buy it? The reason investors pay wholesalers is because they find deals. More agents should look at it from this point of view. I also learned in my years in Real Estate that the MLS never said zero listings. Regardless of the market ups and downs. The MLS never said zero sales either.

I started my Real Estate career in 1992 at the age of 19. My first 4 years in Real Estate was below average. I earned less than $13,000 each year. My friends were all working in fast food or retail so this income was normal in my circle of friends. The only reason I was even still in business is because I had no debt and minimum living expenses. That all changed during my fifth year in real estate because now I had a daughter, car note and house payment. These were grown man builds on a young man's income. In my fifth year I struggled to keep up with bills and expenses. I worked part time jobs only to realize it was a waste of time to work 3 - 4 days a week to make $160. I could just use this effort to close 1 more deal a month.

I remember it was April of that year and I was picking up my check from the bookkeepers office. I noticed a stack of papers with all the agents' year to date earnings. I noticed that one agent had already earned $80,000 between January 1st - April 30th. "What the hell am I doing?" I said to myself. I was barely paying my bills. I immediately tried to justify why this agent was making so much money. Our market area was the Eastside of Detroit near Morang, Cadieux, and Moross. The average sales price in the area was $35,000. I thought maybe he was selling homes in Grosse Pointe. So I went to the listing and pending board and nope! He was selling the same homes I was. I said maybe it's because he's is Caucasian, again nope! 90% of our clients in the office were African American like me. Then I said maybe it's because he is old, again nope! I had just 4 years less experience than he had. Although he may have a better sphere of influence, I couldn't justify him earning 8x my yearly income in only 4 months.

  Later that year I had less than $80; $50 in the bank, $15 in my pocket and $15 in my gas tank. The reason I count the gas in my tank as an asset is because I would make money dropping off friends at work. Here it was October and I am 2 ½ months behind on my car note. Mr. Kahn from the bank called to make a payment arrangement to avoid a 3rd month of delayed payments. I had 2 deals pending that were scheduled to close the following week so I set the payment date for the following Friday. Of course one of the deals did not close. Now I only have enough money to pay the car payments but not my MichCon gas bill. I had a choice, to pay my car note for 1 month and pay MichCon to avoid gas shutoff or pay the car note in full. I decided to pay MichCon. The reason is that October is the last month that the gas company will be aggressive. During the holidays, I noticed that some of the utility companies are more lenient and willing to negotiate payment plans to avoid shutoff during the winter months. This is something I learned by watching my mother when I was younger.

  Well, next week came as did Mr. Kahn's phone call. He left a voice message stating I had defaulted on the payment plan and he would have to send the sharks out this weekend. You agreed to pay by this Friday and we have not received a payment. I know you need your car to sell Real Estate. I called him to explain that I will pay the other payment within a week but now I was going into another month of a late payment. I made it through to November. It was in November my broker informed me that Floyd Wickman Sweat Hogs class was starting. The cost was just under $700. I didn't have the cash to pay and my broker Gary agreed to pay for the class with the agreement that I would reimburse the company from my upcoming commissions. From November to February I would attend this training once a week. If you did not obtain a listing each week you would have to wear a funny dunce hat during the class.

I had to wear it for one week and I said never again. The instructor asked us to make a goal and place it somewhere we could not forget it.

I needed a roof on my home so I took a photo of my house and went to Perry's and had the photo developed to 6x8 size. I laminated the photo with a hole so I could put it on my Keychain.

I walked around for months with my house on a keychain that could not fit all the way in my pocket. During the training class I listed 17 homes. By March of the following year, I was closing 1 - 2 deals per week. Remember Mr. Kahn, he called me in mid-March to discuss my payments on my car. I was almost caught up. I was late with the March payment and April was approaching. Since I was on a watch list he did not want me to get 1 full month behind again. I said to Mr. Kahn this will be our last time speaking. What I learned in Sweat Hogs I still use today. The tools may change but the skills and results don't. 95% of the class was based on generating listing leads through cold calling. We would open the Bressers directory and call each street from top to bottom with the script. This was before the internet and tools like Mojo Dialer.

I learned that if you list, you live. Anytime I was in a slump or on the rollercoaster that an agent goes through, I could always go back to prospecting for listings. I soon learned that if I would just prospect on a daily basis the highs would be higher and the lows would not be rock bottom. If you read any real estate books for agents, the one thing that will be repeated is that listings are the lifeblood of the business. In 2007, we started seeing signs of the market changing. By 2010 it was in deep water. During these years I was at the height of my career up to that point, due to the fact I jumped into the REO market. In 2005 - 2007 I had a few REO contracts but nothing like what would come. Investors would buy and flip in 2005 – 2008, but soon after when the market crashed, it was more difficult to flip but the amount of inventory and low home prices attracted more investors. I decided to pursue more bank REO listing contracts.

In 2013, we started noticing a decrease in REO listing due to the banks being proactive in foreclosure prevention and offering homeowners incentives for Short Sales. During this time, I put more focus on short sales. Due to the overhead and expenses of listing and managing REO properties, short sales seemed like a better option. For example, in order to make money in the REO business in my area, you had to have 20 or more listings each month due to the low price points of the listings. The banks paid a minimum of $1000 to the listing agent. This was 95% of my business since most of the homes in the area were selling below $20,000. The issue was the banks I worked for at the time required we pay for utilities, city inspections, trash out (removal of debris and furniture left by the former owner), lock changes, boarding/securing the properties. It was often that I would have a $12,000 home listed with a $1000 commission but my expenses would be $2000 for utilities, $295 for city inspection, $1000 for trash out, and $150 for lock change. I would earn $1000 but spend $3000+. The banks would reimburse us within 30 - 45 days.

It was like we were loaning money to the bank interest free. This did not include the cost of additional employees to help with the processing and bi-weekly inspection requirements that some of the banks had. It was money to be made and it was profitable when done correctly. But I learned that it only made sense if you could list 20+ homes a month. I would average 350-400 listings per year once I listed homes for some of the larger banks and HUD. HUD was great because we did not have the upfront expenses as with some of the other accounts we had during this time. During this time I learned that systems are a must in order to perform on a high level. This was the first time I read the E-Myth. Then the REO business dried up within 1 year. I went from listing 20 - 30 homes a month to receiving 1 - 2 listings every 3 months.

Banks for example had so many listings before that they outsourced to asset management companies. It was normal to be a listing agent for 4 asset management companies that handled REOs for the same bank. I noticed some of these companies just going out of business within months. This was due to the banks increasing their short sale departments and decreasing the time it took to process and close on short sales. In addition, the market values were increasing and we have seen that the banks were not as aggressive in the foreclosure process as they were in the previous years. In 2014, we saw signs of the market recovery at a speedy rate with values increasing by 25 - 40% per year in some areas. Both short sales and REO were far and few. I went back to basic prospecting for listings. But there was a sector of listing leads I realized would bring in new listings weekly. These were the past buyers who purchased when the market was down. Not every home buyer who purchased during that time was ready to sell. Until they saw what their home was worth. This was also key for investors who paid $80,000 for a home and made $100,000 in rent in the past 5 years and now the home is worth $135,000. This is a whole new market of potential sellers.

Chapter 2
Hunting and Fishing

In real estate you are either sowing seeds for future business or Hunting and Fishing for the immediate return. Let's take a further look.

Hunting - is going after FSBO and expired listings. This is a sitting target you have to aim for with the proper skills. But advertising to buyers and sellers is similar to fishing. You place an ad in a sea of potential leads hoping to catch one. The quality and quantity of leads you catch is based on the bait you use. Sowing seeds is different. For example, a farmer may plant seeds and expect them to grow over a period of time. That same farmer may have to hunt for food now.

Fishing - Advertising and marketing is a form of fishing where you are placing ads as bait to catch potential buyers and sellers. Sometimes you get more than your boat can hold. Sometimes you get nothing. Sometimes you catch what you want and throw the rest back, well not actually throw them back. Because in real estate, we just refer the extra leads to someone else. Just like fishing you don't just go and place your ads anywhere. You place your ads based on the type of business you want. There are different leads in the ocean than the lake. For seller leads, you may advertise an expensive home for sale. The higher up in price the more likely that buyer may have a home to sell. You may do online or social media squeeze pages that offer free home value reports. You may advertise cash for homes allowing you to purchase homes as-is or fix and flip them on the market. When someone calls you to sell their home as-is you have two options, to list it as-is or buy it.

The Expired Listing Myth

Although 70 - 90% of expired listings are motivated, not all are ready to re-list immediately. Keep in mind some sellers who have expired were just testing the market and wanted a price that was high enough to motivate them to move now. This would explain the lack of price reductions on the listing. Either the listing agent could not convince them to reduce the price or they never really wanted to sell the home for its current market value. Some of these sellers had life changes that caused them to stay, and no amount of money would solve the problem, so they decided to stay put. Here is the good news. All your expired listing scripts work! Just not right now. If you practice and go after expired listings this is a good way to get listings but what about the other 30% or 10% (depending on your area and market conditions) that did not relist right away? You have to use a long term nurture approach with them. See, most agents will hunt these sellers but not have a follow up plan 3 months, 6 months, or even 1 year from now when the seller's motivation returns.

If you are a new agent or never worked expired listings here is an example.

Let's say the homeowner was considering relocating to another state for a job opportunity in the company. They decided to list the home. The spouse stayed here while the home was on the market while the other spouse went away to test the new job and state for 60 days. During this time the spouse realized that the move was lateral and not an improvement, the new position was not better, the new city, the new schools, etc. If the current home had sold they would have stuck with the commitment to relocate. But since the home did not sell it was convenient to just move back home and take the house off the market. Most agents would forget about this seller. During your initial call you should be able to determine the motivation beyond the job opportunity. There was something that made them want to move in the first place but the motivation was not strong enough at the time. Maybe 3, 6, 12, or even 24 months from now they will be willing to sell. What realtor will they choose? Probably the one that called to see how things are going, sent market updates, invited them to client events and built rapport.

FSBOs

Have you ever called a FSBO and used a FSBO script? You know the question that says how long are you going to try selling your home before you hire a Realtor? The seller answers you by saying they already have a Realtor in mind. Of course you can still get this listing. There are books, coaches and scripts that will teach you all the techniques on how to get this listing anyway. My question is how did the agent get there FIRST? Did the agent have any FSBO training? Maybe not. If so, this seller probably would have never listed the home as a FSBO. This is why you need to understand how to Hunt, Fish and Sow Seeds. In order to last in the business you have to be able to close deals now.

Agents who have mastered the skills of converting FSBOs have a unique talent that most agents will never master. It's called follow up. Most FSBO's are not stingy with rejection. They have enough rejection to pass out to everybody. They say "No, Not Interested", "I'll sell it myself", "I don't want to pay a commission", "I have an attorney", "Realtors suck", and etc. In a good sellers' market, with low inventory, FSBOs have the better chance of selling their home without an agent. The issue now becomes closing the deal.

The Direct Approach to FSBOs

This is a direct approach using scripts and follow up calls, direct mail, marketing and visits to the property until the seller decides to list with you or another agent. Visiting the home is the most effective in some cases but it is time consuming. You must list follow up for 6-8 weeks on average to convert most FSBO's. Most FSBOs will list with a realtor after 6 weeks. The only reasons a FSBO will not list is either because they cannot afford to hire an agent due to a high mortgage balance and limited equity in the home, they sold the home, or they were not really motivated to sell and were just testing the market.

The Transaction Coordinator Approach to FSBOs

Some agents decide to not ask for the listings directly but instead offer other services to FSBOs like offering to be a transaction coordinator for a flat fee if the seller secures a buyer. This is more of a passive approach to FSBOs and not as effective and profitable. But I have noticed agents turn this into a relationship and turn this into a listing.

There are pros and cons to this approach. The disadvantage would be if the deal starts going bad and you and the seller are not in line with beliefs on how to get to the closing table. If the deal does not close the seller may see you in a negative way and not hire you once they decide to list the home. This is natural; some people see a negative experience and place everybody that was part of the experience in a negative part of their memory. For example, someone who had a bad experience their first time at the dentist may associate the person at the front desk, the assistant, the building and everything and everyone associated with the dentist as part of that experience.

The advantage, on the other hand, is if the deal does close. You can now market that you assisted with the sale of the property to all the other homeowners in the area. Whenever I act as a transaction coordinator on any deal, not just FSBOs, I also obtain permission to list the home in the MLS and mark it pending and sold. Check your local board and MLS requirements when doing this. The reason I do this is because I am able to market for more listings based on my sales in the area. It's like a big announcement saying the FSBO had their sign in the yard but still used the service of an agent. That agent was me. Just like you would announce you sold a coop agent listing, you would do the same with a FSBO. Every homeowner you can afford to market to in that neighborhood needs to know your involvement in the sale.

The Loan Officer Approach

Here is a sample script a loan rep can use. "Hello this is John Doe loan rep over at ABC Loans. I noticed your home is listed for sale. Do you mind if I market your home to our list of pre-approved buyers? Do you have a lender to qualify your buyers during your open house? If you don't mind, I can come to your next open house and qualify buyers who are interested in buying a home. This will make sure you're not signing a contract with a buyer who is not able to obtain a loan." (Side note - I don't use the words sign contract with my clients but in this case I would use those words. This lets the seller know they are entering into a binding contract with a buyer)

If the seller is not having an open house, the loan rep should offer to help coordinate an open house.

The reason I mention this is because this should be your loan rep that you have referred business to over the years. The loan rep can obtain clients and possibly refer them to several realtors. One of them would be you. If one of the buyers likes the FSBOs home your loan rep can suggest the seller hire an attorney or broker to help with the transaction. The loan rep can refer them to several attorneys or agents who offer transaction coordination services. Again, you should be on that list.

Probate Sellers

The truth is there are new probate opportunities coming to the market every day. When a homeowner dies and there is real estate as part of the estate, this can become a burden on the heirs or it can solve their financial problems. Let's face it, most people do not prepare for death.

Just ask your family and friends who own a home if they have a will or trust. You will be surprised. For most of them, the home is their most valuable asset. When someone dies, the family has to deal with two things.

1. Settling all the financial issues
2. Settling all the family issues that are caused by financial issues

In addition, the family still has to deal with the death of a loved one. If there is no will or trust that gives detailed instructions, the family will most likely deal with probate for months. What happens to the home during this time? Also, the bills don't stop coming for the home because the owner died. Families may fight over the bank account, personal property and the home. If they cannot agree sometimes the court will determine the solution for them. This sometimes includes selling the home. In some cases, selling the home will solve all the financial issues with the estate. You need to find the executor or personal representative and introduce yourself. DO NOT ask for the listing during your first call/letter. This is also why you need to build relationships with attorneys in your area that handle probate cases.

Each probate case is different. You will have clients that are not at all emotionally tied to the home and then you will have some that will be so emotionally attached that they will leave the property vacant for months or years just to avoid letting go. Some families have no need for the money but they will want to get the process over with. On the other hand, you have families that are in desperate need of the funds from the sale of the home.

With probate you will deal not only with selling the home but you have to be prepared to deal with all the family disputes that may arise. Just like divorce listings you will need to avoid taking sides with one of the family members.

Probate marketing will include a direct mail campaign, online advertising, and telephone prospecting. The direct mail campaign should offer services and resources other than listing the home. Offer resources like referrals for estate sale reps and companies, contractors, debris removal and clean out companies. These vendors can help you secure a relationship with the client even if you do not list the home.

Divorced sellers

Some of the most motivated sellers are clients going through divorce. They are often given a date that they must list or sell the home. There are times when one spouse will simply buy out the other spouse's equity in the home. But in most cases the home is sold. I noticed that either one or both parties don't want to stay in the home for emotional reasons. In some cases, both parties may want to keep the home but can't decide who shall keep it so the court orders a sale. The most common is when neither spouse can afford to keep the home on one income. Think about all the buyers you have sold homes to. Most of your single buyers purchased within their individual budget. Most of your buyers who have a partner or spouse are more likely to purchase a home based on a two income household budget. Even if one of them doesn't qualify individually, buyers will budget their home purchase based on having two incomes to cover the home expenses. With that being said, these can become highly motivated sellers or the court will order the sale of the home for financial reasons. Anytime the court orders a sale, this is the highest motivation you can find.

So how do you find divorced sellers? Some divorce filings are public record and posted in local legal news publications. The best way to connect with these types of seller leads is to connect with divorce attorneys. You will need to prospect divorce attorneys the same way you would a seller lead. You can also run ads for divorce sellers looking to liquidate a home in the most convenient way.

When finding someone going through divorce, how will you convince both parties to hire you as their listing agent? When speaking to one party, you must not take sides. You should prospect both parties and interview with both parties, even if it's a separate time. Your goal is to build rapport and trust with both sellers to show that you are able to sell their home. Remember that in some cases, the home is the only thing holding up the process to move on.

I sold a home to a couple back in 2011 for $125,000. In 2017 we sold the home for $205,000 during their divorce. This couple had a combined household income of just under $95,000. Both parties could afford to keep the home individually. The issue at the time was that they had a terrible divorce that cost them a combined total of $57,000 in attorney fees. Neither party could afford to pay the attorney fees in one lump fund out of pocket. The solution was to sell the home.

This is just one example of how every divorce is different.

Absentee Owners

Absentee owners are typically owners who live outside of the city or state in which the property is located. The most common absentee owners are investors and vacation homeowners. Some probate sellers will fall into this category also. The probate absentee owners are actually some of the most motivated of all sellers. This is especially true for someone who inherited a home in an area that is not desirable.

Absentee owners' motivation can change with the market conditions and economic shifts. For example, when someone owns a vacation home when the economy is in distress, this vacation home can be considered an unnecessary asset similar to a boat or other expensive toys. When the economy is distressed, some investors may sell some or their entire investment portfolio due to tenants not being able to pay rent due to economic conditions. After all, they purchased the investments to generate income when needed. On the opposite end, when the economy is booming some investors may decide to sell some or all of their portfolio due to the increase of appreciation of value. **It's basically buy low, hold, rent for cash flow, and sell high**. When these investors sell these properties at the new increased values they are often looking to invest the money into other larger properties like multifamily or commercial. This is when understanding how 1031 exchanges work will help you earn more business.

You can find absentee owners through a number of resources and online services. You can find the name, telephone number, and email address to most of the absentee owners. If the property is owned by the seller's corporation or LLC then you may have to check state records to find the mailing address for the company. Finding absentee owners who own properties in their Self Directed IRA can be difficult. Most of the mailing addresses will list the custodian.

Bank Foreclosures/REO

REO or Real Estate Owned is what banks call their foreclosed homes. In order to become a listing agent for foreclosures, you will need to connect with asset managers or asset management companies. Asset managers usually are responsible for overseeing the process of selling the properties, reviewing offers and approving repairs and expenses on the properties. In other words, the asset manager is your seller. There are several types of foreclosures and REO properties based on the type of loan that was originated.

There are several types of repossessed and bank foreclosures you can list. Keep in mind that some entities will only sign the master listing agreement with the broker of the office. The broker can then assign the listings to a designated agent in the office.

Asset managers will require you to use their forms for purchasing. There will be guidelines you need to follow such as biweekly inspections, monthly reports or BPOs (broker price opinions).

Some asset managers will test your knowledge of the market by requesting you complete BPOs on several properties prior to them hiring you to list any homes.

You can apply with asset management companies online or attend some of the REO conferences. Some organizations like NAREB (National Association of Real Estate Brokers) and others have asset managers who attend their events for networking and provide education on how to list and sell their assets.

Another option for foreclosures is to check with your local municipality to see if they have a Land Bank or something similar. Local cities and counties often have homes they need to sell, either through auction or listing with an agent. Also don't forget local credit unions and smaller local banks also have REO properties.

Pre-foreclosures/Short Sales

These are the most motivated when speaking of solutions, but these are not always the most motivated to sell. Here is what I mean. When someone is facing foreclosure they need to either save the home or sell to prevent damage to their credit, embarrassment, and devastation of losing a home.

Not all sellers care to sell their home to prevent foreclosure. You can easily find pre foreclosures in your local county records. Depending on your state, most foreclosure notices are posted in some type of legal news publication. By law, there has to be some form of notice to the general public. This alerts anyone who may have an interest in the property that it is in foreclosure. There are third party companies who provide this data for a fee.

Chapter 3
The ACTION Items

None of this matters if you don't know what to do. Prospecting is one of the most effective ways to build your business. It is also inexpensive. See, as an agent you will spend time or money to receive leads. Prospecting costs time. This should be the go to action item for new agents with little to no budget for marketing.

Most people are not comfortable prospecting either face to face or on the phone. The truth is we all are natural prospectors. Think back to when you were a teenager or young adult dating. Either you would go to a place like a club, bar, or the area hangout for all the people your age. During this time you were either one of the two types of people. Person 1. You were looking to connect with someone by approaching them or Person 2. You were looking to be approached by someone. If you were person 1, you would dress for the part, you would also practice what you would say, you would play it back in your head before you made your approach and then bam! Rejection. At this point, depending on the type of person you are, you would call it a night or try another prospect. If you were person 2, you would dress the part and make yourself seem approachable, depending on your personality type you may dance to attract attention as if to say "Hey! Look at me! I am available!", you may walk around to make sure you are noticed by everyone in the building, or you may stay in one spot the entire night to because you feel like you can draw enough attention and those confident enough would come to you.

At the end of the night persons 1 and 2 would go come and tally up the amount of contacts made. Both would filter through to see who was a great potential candidate to date in the future. Not everyone will qualify.

Now let's say person 1 and 2 are Realtors. Person 1 is prospecting and Person 2 is advertising.

Grant Cardone has a book titled If You're Not First You're Last. This is why I prefer to use the sowing techniques. I want to be the first person someone thinks of 5 - 7 years before they list their home. It's not likely that there are several techniques used to build future leads.

Prospecting solves problems; your problems and your clients'. The best way to think about prospecting is to think that at this moment there is someone looking to list their home on the market soon. You have to believe that you are the best person to help them with their situation. The problem is that they do not currently know you. You want them to have the best chance for success.

Action Items

1. **Circle prospecting**
2. **Farming**
3. **Current and Past buyers**
4. **Retired agents**

1. Circle Prospecting

Circle prospecting is basically calling, mailing, or door knocking in an area in which a listing is sold, active or pending. You have probably heard it several times, that when one listing sells others will follow. Curious neighbors are sometimes surprised at what the shabby house down the street sold for. Even if the home sold was not shabby, everyone thinks their home is better than the one sold. DO NOT wait for them to call another agent to find out the value of their home. Let's say you are not the listing agent for the home sold, you can still inform neighbors of market data of homes sold in the area. If you are the buyers' agent of the home that sold you should always notify the neighborhood that you provided the buyer for the home.

For example, "I'm Jane Doe Realtor I want to introduce you to your newest neighbors, the Smiths, whom I helped become homeowners in your neighborhood. I have other families looking to move into your area. If you are considering selling in the near future, please feel free to contact me. "

This works for pending sales also. Just change sold to pending/under contract

2. Farming

Farming is selecting an area to market to on a consistent basis over the course of a year. If you are going to farm an area, do it big or don't do it at all. You may just waste your money. There are several steps to selecting a farm area.

Step 1. Determine the conversion rate for the area. Find out how many homes are in the neighborhood's farm area. Check the MLS to see how many homes sold in the past 12 months. Check pending and listings also to get an idea of the amount of current activity in the area.

Step 2. Check for a dominant agent. If there is an agent with 20% or more of the market share, determine if you have what it takes to take market share from this agent or at least compete for the other business. Remember a dominant agent that was first to this area will be more difficult to dominate in this farm. But even the dominant agent had to start somewhere. If the dominant agent has been in the business more than 15 years, you may find out the agent is coasting and is used to not having competition in the area. He or she may not use the latest technology and may feel they do not need to give any more effort to maintain the farm.

Step 3. Build a website and/or social media page named after the farm area. If the area does not have a name, GIVE it one. Information should be posted that is unique to your area. The online platform should be promoted in your mailers

Step 4. Mail to the farm on a monthly basis.

Farming is more than an area. You can farm to a demographic or a niche market. For example absentee owners, seniors who need to downsize their home, or people who need larger homes. You can market to a group of people based on their needs.

3. Current and past clients.

Your buyers are your FUTURE SELLERS. This is like having a fruit tree that you can eat from anytime you want. Any good Real Estate coach or Trainer will tell you to work your database. Each client on average provides you with 7 referrals within 10 years. Then each of those 7 people will provide you with 7 more referrals each. Look at the following Diagram.

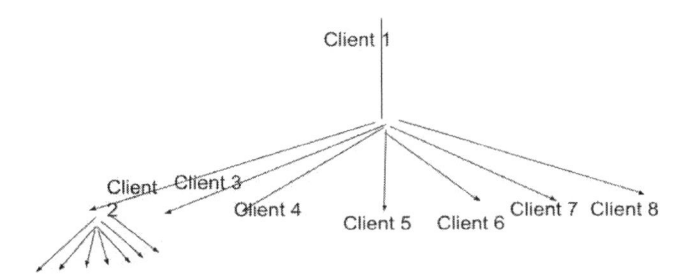

Let's say that your average commission is $6,000. What is your first client worth?
8 x $6000 = $48,000 on the first level.
56 x $6000 = $336,000 on the second level.

So now imagine that you start out with 12 clients your first year. Your second level would be over $4,032,000.00 That is only 1 client closing a month for one year. Can you close 12 deals a year? Of course. The problem is that most agents will not realize the second and third level client referrals. Some agents will have second level referrals within 3 years and some in 10 years. Let's say it takes 10 years to turn those 12 clients into second level referrals. That would give you over $400,000 a year in commission income from referrals. If you do it in 3 years, that would give you over $1,300,000.00 a year in commission income. 7 - 10 years from now, the original 12 clients start buying and selling again. Then the process starts all over again.

Now imagine if an older agent or broker came to you with the above database of clients for the past 10 years and said I will sell you my database of clients along with my brand name for $500,000. The agent allowed you to pay them in yearly payments of $100,000 per year. Would you purchase it? Your answer should be YES! Depending on the average commission amount. This is called a Book of Business. Business owners pay money for this all the time. Your job is to grow your business in order to grow your book of business.

Let's say I offered to sell you a business for $500,000 and you could yearn $300,000 a year or an apartment building for $500,000 with $3,500,000 profit over 10 years. So how do you build your client database to generate referrals 2 - 5 levels deep? It's a system for how you generate repeat and referral business. Below are some of the strategies used to stay top of mind with your past clients.

Client Events

Since the impact of Covid-19 crisis, social gatherings may be limited. But overall, client events are one of the most profitable things an agent can do. You can find ways to have virtual gatherings. During times when people are comfortable, you can rent a movie theater, bowling alley, etc. and invite your clients for FREE. The benefit of doing this allows you to connect with your clients 3 - 4 months before the event.

For example, you are having a client event in June. In February, you send an invitation and make a phone call. In March, you send an Eventbrite and/or email invite. In April, you call and email. In May you send another mail invite. You have connected with the client several times in 4 months. The message you want to send is that I appreciate you so much as a client that I am giving you and your family a FREE experience. But guess what some of your customers are thinking? "Hey, my agent is still in Real Estate and doing so well that they can afford to rent an entire theater, bowling alley, etc."

No matter how many times I have done events, someone always assumes that I spent a lot of money on the event and I am doing well because I spent a lot of money to invite them to something like this. This is one of the most impressive things an agent can do. Agents can get creative with events and also have different themed events for different family members. Like a ladies night event, a man cave event or events for the kids. My suggestion is to think of events from the customer point of view not yours. All your clients will not like all the events and that's fine but they will eventually attend one of them if you are consistent.

If you partner with vendors and affiliates like mortgage companies, home inspectors, etc. make sure to allow them to invite some of their clients. These are orphan buyers and potential future clients of yours. Most of the people they invite have forgotten their realtors already. If the loan rep that they trust with their finances introduces you as one of their realtors and they attend your future events. It is likely they will call you when it's time to sell.

Pop-bys

An agent on my team, Chandra Graves, was buying these corny looking tea bags and I asked what she was doing with them. She said "I am mailing them to my clients." She described the item with a corny phrase like have a Tea-Riffic day. We both laughed. My first thought was that this is corny. She drives by her clients homes and drops off similar items. She has mastered this to the point that one of our clients sent an invite to their wedding. She got an invite and I didn't (relationship) that's what this is all about. Her personality is great and along with Pop-bys in her arsenal, she is great at keeping top of mind with past clients. Don't let her meet your past client. LOL. She showed me one Brian Buffini video on the subject and I was fully convinced. 2 months later I was in the cold snow storm dropping off small buckets of rock salt. (If you don't know, in Michigan, we use rock salt to melt the ice on our walkways and driveways). One of my clients recorded a video then, posted it on social media showing the whole world my bucket of salt that she appreciated, showing my card on the bucket. Boom (relationship).

Chapter 4
The Birds and the Seeds

I once heard Jim Rohn talk about sowing seeds in a speech. What I remember most is that he mentioned that the birds will get some of the seeds. I thought about this in my Real Estate business. Some seeds will fall on soil that is not fertile. Think of your potential clients as soil.

Soil = Area, Clients, and Leads
Seeds = Marketing and Advertising
Harvest = Listings, Buyer, Closings, and Commissions

Let's look at the following examples.

Soil - You run ads or start a marketing campaign to attract leads. The target audience or area you are promoting to may not give you the results you want. The ads or marketing may not have been planted in the right type of soil or during the ideal time. If you are running ads to attract Short Sales listings but the market is not currently distressed. You may have planted a good seed in the wrong soil.

Birds - In this case, birds are anything that interferes with the seeds you planted. Let's say you run an ad or campaign that is trend-setting and the leads are coming in. You start to notice copycat ads by other agents. Their ads are similar to yours. Some of these agents have bigger budgets and even improved on your ad and now your percentage of market share is decreasing. Or maybe you are known in one area as the agent of choice. Now there is a new agent that has entered the market and taken market share. These are both examples of birds swooping in and taking the seeds you planted. One major bird is the local and national media. Have you ever noticed that the media seems to be 3 - 6 months behind when it comes to the real estate market? This is because the media needs to see a trend before they report it. For example, let's say it's December and homes are selling in 1 - 3 days with multiple offers. This trend goes on for 6 months. Buyers start complaining how difficult it is to purchase a home due to the competition. The media starts reporting this in October. By then, the market is starting to shift to a more balanced market but your sellers still believe that their home will sell in 2 days. The media's influence may impact when your sellers' decide to list and for what price.

We have to live with the fact that there will be all types of birds coming into our market or attracting our current and past clients. The fact is you can't protect all your seeds but you have to do a good job of nurturing the seeds you have planted.

Harvest - When you plant certain seeds in the correct soil you reap the benefits again without as much effort required when you first planted the seeds. For example, let's say you run an ad for 6 months and you were spending $500 per month. During this time you have become known in the area. Let's say you look at your ROI and number of leads and realize that you can adjust the ad and spend $350 to get the same results. Not only have you lowered your expenses you can attract better leads due to tracking and adjusting the ad based on past results. You will also notice that some of the leads that did not buy or list several months ago are calling you eight to ten months later. All from efforts you made months ago.

In real estate, you will have birds all around your potential listing. Your past clients or people in your database may receive mail, phone calls, email and etc. from you on a regular basis. For some reasons out of your control they will still list or buy with someone else.

Remember that client you drove around with for 5 months showing homes. Then they stopped looking only to call you back 3 months later to start looking again. This time they made offers only to get out bid on everything so they put it off again. 2 months later they call you to inquire about a home that does not match any of their needs. Then finally they make an offer and it gets accepted. During the process you have to negotiate everything under the sun. You even have to throw in part of your commission to get both parties to agree on concessions. Well, 7 years go by and you are in the neighborhood, you drive by and boom. It is a for sale sign in the yard. How did this happen? You have to understand this is just as much your fault as anything. You have to stay in front of your past clients on a regular basis. Your goal is to be top of mind and first in mind to all of your past clients regardless of your experience with this client.

      This also happens to people that you have met during your prospecting. Imagine you look in the MLS and see a new listing. Not just any listing, it is the homeowner you have been nurturing for 2 years via telephone. So what happened? You let the birds get them. See you planted the seed but you may have failed at building rapport in which the homeowner either trusts that you are the best for the job or you did not build a good enough top of mind so the owner may have forgotten you.

Chapter 5
Tools and Skills

Listing presentations are the armor you need and the fire extinguisher you will need (break glass when needed). It surprises me how many agents do not have a listing presentation. Not a fancy digital one, but just none at all. Let's look at it this way. A listing is your castle and your yard sign is the flag to mark your territory. Once a seller invites you into the castle your job is to post your flag. You must have all the tools and weapons to fortify and protect yourself from enemy attacks of other agents who also have appointments with the seller. Your listing presentation should include your marketing plan, your resume, and objection handlers.

During your presentation you need to show the sellers three things 1. How much can you sell the home for? 2. How long it will take and 3. How will you do it? Everything else in your presentation is to handle objections. Your listing presentation should be presented to the seller based on their personality type. You can study DISC or other similar personality exercises to understand your clients. Your presentation should include everything even if you don't need it.

For example, your Aunt calls you to list her home. She is ready to sell, you know where she is moving, you know all the information, she trusts you, and she knows what price she wants. The price she wants for the home is within the market range for the area. You show up with just a listing agreement. She proceeds to ask you details about market times, stats, types of buyer financing and more. Her friend told her about a bad experience with repairs and closing costs. As she is asking these questions she shows you some things she read. You don't have any data or information prepared to show her. She needs to see visuals that support what you are saying.

She asks if she can sign the papers another day. Believe it or not this happens all the time and in this case the aunt now has some doubts. Nothing is worse than having sellers call you out to their home and you show up only to not get the listing after months of nurturing this client.

You have to develop an arsenal to obtain listing leads. You need a balance of the right tools and skills. If you lack skills you need to have tools that will provide you a large number of leads. This will cost you either money or time. If you have a high skill set you will want as many quality leads you can obtain. As an experienced agent, you can be more selective of the leads you target. This is usually true because an experienced agent will know where to go for the highest return on his/her time and efforts. An experienced agent will base his/her efforts on their goals for the year. If an 18 year old learned to use a hunting rifle 1 week ago and you took him or her out hunting for the first time, then placed 100 deer within 20 feet of the hunter, it's likely the hunter would hit a deer. If you have a hunter with 30 years of experience, take them hunting with no deer on site for miles. This hunter would know where to sit and set up their equipment, they would probably have some types of gadgets to attract deer; they would have on camouflage to hide from the deer. In some cases the hunter may not see any deer for 4 - 6 hrs. But guess what, even though the hunter may see only 1 - 2 deer a day, the hunter would have enough skill to hit its target even if they only have an opportunity at one shot.

Chapter 6
Is it the Seed or the Soil?

The first question agents ask is where do I start? My answer is anywhere you plan to finish. You can start with a small neighborhood or an entire zip code, an entire city or a county. This will have more to do with the amount of effort and money you're able to invest. The more you grow your business you can spread out over a larger area. But this is not just about the area, sometimes you are sowing seeds in a select group of people. For example, you may research several areas in which the average age of the homeowner is above 60 years of age. The average home size is 2300 sqft and the average home style is 2-story colonial. It does not take rocket science to know that some of these people will need to downsize. This group of people should know who you are 5 - 7 years before they even consider selling.

How do you know when it is time to stop or change strategies? There are times when you may be doing all the correct actions but in the wrong area. Or you are working in a neighborhood farm area but have had no results. This is when tracking your activities and expenses are very important. While one approach may take you one year to see any results another may take eighteen months or more. You may farm two separate areas using the same strategy but get completely different results. You may run an ad to attract sellers on Facebook and realize the wording in one ad generates more results than a similar ad with the same target market.

Every strategy and approach will require a 6 month to 2 year commitment to test and adjust. This is the only way you will even have enough results to track and compare. In every market, there are successful agents that are using similar strategies and approaches that you can study and track to see what is working.

Chapter 7
Harvest your crops

All the efforts you have done so far to get leads are useless if you cannot convert them into listings. There are several steps to making sure you increase your chances of listing a home.

1. **Setting bona fide appointments**
2. **Listing presentation**
3. **Database follow up**

1. Setting bona fide appointments

It is very important when you are setting appointments that you are increasing your chances to list the home during the first visit. Avoid going on appointments that do not have all of the following:

1. All decision makers will be present at the appointment
2. They actually want to sell
3. They know what price they want
4. They are motivated and not just selling out of convenience

Decision Makers

No matter what is said on the phone conversation, never schedule confirmation without both decision makers home. When you only meet with one party, your chances increase of having to schedule a 2nd and possibly a 3rd appointment just to get a listing. There are times when you may still schedule an appointment. Let's say the sellers are relocating out of town for a new job. The wife has already moved to start working and the husband is staying at the home until it sells. You may meet with the husband and wife signs electronically. This type of appointment is good because the motivation is high.

There are times when you will go on an appointment and not obtain the listing because the seller wants to interview other agents or the seller is not in a position to list the home at this time. A strong listing presentation will help increase your chances even in these situations.

They Want to Sell

This may seem obvious but there are hundreds of sellers who just want a market evaluation with no intention to sell. They may want an evaluation to help them determine value due to divorce, refinance, or other reasons in which the owner(s) may need to know the market value of the home. They may choose to have an agent/broker evaluation instead of paying for an appraisal. The good news is that these people can go into your database for a potential future listing. The best way to determine the seller's intention is to ask the right questions on the phone before setting the appointment. Ask questions like, "When do you need to sell?", "Why are you selling?"

They Know What Price They Want

Most people have a price in mind but will not tell you over the phone. The reason being is they want your honest evaluation without any influence. This is mostly the case when a seller is not sure if the price they want is too low and they fear that they may be taken advantage of. Most sellers who are confident or even have high expectations of their home's market value, have no problem telling you the price they want. These sellers have usually done some research.

Here is a common conversation I have with sellers.

Agent: How much would you like to sell your home for?
Seller: I don't know; I was hoping you could suggest a price when you come to see it?

Agent: That's fine. May I ask, have you made major improvements in the past 5 years?
Seller: Yes we updated the kitchen?
Agent: That's great. That will be a good selling feature. How much did you invest in the updates?
Seller: We spent over $40,000 and we put on a new roof about 10 years ago
Agent: How long have you lived in the home?
Seller: 15 years
Agent: That was a good time to buy. May I ask how much you purchased the home for?
Seller: $200,000.
Agent: That's great. So we want to make sure you are not losing money sounds like we want to sell for close to $290,000 or more correct
Seller: Yes

At this point the seller may even give you a higher sales price. The reason I ask this question is because if the seller's ideal price is not realistic you may have to decide if you want to schedule the listing appointment or not. If you believe that you can convince the seller to list at fair market value during your presentation go ahead and schedule an appointment. If you believe the seller is not going to be realistic in pricing, you may not want to schedule an appointment and just send a market evaluation.

They are Motivated and Not Just Selling out of Convenience

To be honest, some people will list just to see if the home sells. These types of sellers are more likely to be overpriced or have so many contingencies that it may not be worth the time and effort to list the home. These often end up on the expired or withdrawn list. When another agent calls them to relist, they usually say they are going to wait until next year or some other far out time to sell. This is because the true motivation was not there. Do not confuse monetary motivation with convenience. Some sellers are selling only because the market is hot and they can profit a large amount by selling now. Although this is convenient, the true motivation is the money they will make from the home.

2. Listing Presentation

We covered this in chapter 5.

3. Database Follow-up

In this case, we are referring to following up on listing leads. Agents often go on listing appointments with no follow-up plan in mind. For example, seller calls you and responds to your free home evaluation ad. After going on the appointment, you realize that the seller doesn't have plans to list and sell the property until 7 months to a year from now. Most agents don't put this lead into any database or follow-up system. Only to ride past the home 7 months later to see it listed with another realtor. Without a follow-up plan for every listing appointment, agents are likely to miss out on plenty of opportunity to list with sellers who may not list for several months or years down the line.

Chapter 8
Marketing (Not Prospecting)

In today's world, you can have mass webinars for buyers and sellers. Since people have become more comfortable with virtual meetings and group chats, people are more open to virtual presentations. Everyone will eventually start hosting home buyer and home seller webinars online. If not, they will at least try it for some time. Marketing is an **INVESTMENT** in your business. You will eventually need to market for seller leads to leverage your time. Marketing is your way of reaching a large number of potential sellers that you would not be able to speak to in person or over the phone in a short period of time.

The issue with marketing is that what works now will not work the same in the future. You will have to adjust your marketing as the market shifts or competition crowds the space. For example, when squeeze pages and landing pages first hit the internet it was easy to simply place a "What's your Home Worth" post or ad and get potential seller leads. Now you can run this ad and it will still work but nothing like it did in 2013. Prospecting will always keep you in tune with what's going on in the market by speaking directly with clients. Marketing will increase the number of clients you can get. Even when you prospect, you will have to market to your potential clients you have from prospecting.

The two most important things you will need to set are:

1. A marketing budget and
2. Return on investment goal.

You will need to stay within your budget. Most agents make the mistake of setting a budget that they cannot maintain for 12 months. This is very important because most of the marketing you do will take 3, 6, 9, or 12 months to give results that you can track and may take 6 - 12 months to show a return on investment.

Chapter 9
Hire, Invest, and Profit

Just like separating your business bank account from your personal bank account, **I honestly believe each agent should separate their business into two divisions: Listings and Buyers.** You should have a system or spreadsheet that shows your P and L (profit and loss) for your listing business and your buyer business.

We often commingle our overall profit from other sources to help fund a failing division. For example, when I first became a HUD listing broker, I had several upfront expenses required by the asset manager. I had to increase staff, have a minimum of 100 signs that met HUD guidelines and more. All this before I had 1 listing. I was able to fund these expenses because my business from other clients like Banks and private retail sellers was profitable. I had 9 different bank clients and HUD. I was able to see how much money I spent in utilities, landscaping, and locksmiths for each bank client. I was also able to see which client accounts were not profitable. This allowed me to end those client relationships. Although I was making money with them, it was not enough profit for the time and energy needed to cover my other expenses such as staff.

This is going to help you turn down all the solicitors trying to sell you the latest bells and whistles. You need our Lead system, you need our Website, You need our CRM, and you need and so on and so on.

PRO TIP- Never ever buy an ad to boost your ego.

Advertisers know that agents have huge egos and will buy ads with their name and face on them, even if the ad performs poorly. Ask yourself what attracts more buyers?

Information and photos of homes or information and photos of agents? If you don't know, ask Zillow to remove all their homes and advertise agents only.

Regardless of the **business** you are building, you will eventually need to leverage your time. There are hundreds of books on team building and management. I recommend reading the E-Myth and The Millionaire Real Estate agent.

The simple way to explain it is that you want to replace yourself by starting with the task that you either don't like doing or the task that you are not good at. You will either have to be average and hire great people, or become great and hire great people. Either way, you need great people. Only a **GREAT SYSTEM** will allow you to hire *average* people. The overall goal is to build a business that makes a **profit**. Whether you are an individual agent, team leader, or broker the focus should be profit first.

Listings offer the best use of time, money and leveraged marketing. Therefore, listings offer the best potential for a profitable business. To increase your leverage with buyers, you will eventually want to hire a buyer's agent or showing agent to assist you. It will only make sense if you have enough listings that you can market and attract an overflow of buyer leads. If you were to hire a buyer's agent and had to pay for leads, this will decrease your profit percentage overall. This due to the fact that marketing a listing is usually always cheaper than any third party buyer leads. Why do you think Zillow and Realtor.com market **LISTINGS**?

Let's look at a few examples:

1. The first example assumes you have an admin.
   - Paid 3rd party leads like Zillow or Realtor.com. Let's say you sign up for a 6 month contract and you're paying $800 per month for leads.
   - $800 x 6 = $4800

- Let's say you receive 24 buyer leads (3 per month).
- You convert 3 of them to actual buyers.
- You put 21 in your database and set on a drip campaign for future business.
- Your average price point is $200,000.
- Your buy side commission is 3%.
- Your total commission for each buyer is $6,000.
- You earn $18,000.
- $4800 invested to earn $18,000, with additional potential buyers in your database for future income.
- At first glance this would seem like a fair ROI (return on investment) of your $4800. Let's break this down and look at actual numbers that would show on a P and L (profit and loss statement)

- $18,000 Gross
- $4800 Ad
- $12,000 Admin assistant (his could range from $2000 - $4000 per month)
- $1200 Net profit.
- If you have a buyer's agent/showing assistant this would further decrease your profit.
- This has not even taken into consideration your broker split, or if you are a broker this does not include your office overhead.

With this example, you only have several options.

1. Increase your skill set to convert more of the 24 leads.
2. Spend more to generate more leads.

The issue with option 2 is the more leads you have the more help you need in the form of an administrative assistant or buyer's agent. This is the dilemma that most agents don't even know they have. They just look at the $18,000 and $4,800.

2. Marketing a listing. Using the same 6 month period. Let's say you receive 10 seller leads you received from a sphere of influence referral or past client by doing the activities

earlier in the book. Let's assume the average listing is $200,000.
- You earn 3% and a co-op broker has the buyer and receives 3%.
- Your total commission is $6,000 per home.
- It is likely your conversion rate would be over 60% since these are past clients or direct referrals. For your example let's say you convert 70%
- 7 listings received. Let's say 70% of these listings will sell within the 6 month period 5.
- 5 x $6,000 = $30,000
- $30,000 Gross
- $500 per month marketing to sphere and past clients via mail, email and calls.
- $500 per month marketing the listings.
- $12,000 Admin assistant (this could range from $2000 - $4000 per month)
- $12,000 Net profit.

Here is the cherry on top. Each listing should generate 7 - 10 buyer leads and of those buyer leads you convert 1 - 3 per month for each listing.
- Let's use 1 buyer lead per month for each listing.
- 7 buyers x 6 months = 42 buyers
- 42 x $6,000 = $252,000
- Now you actually **need** a buyer's agent.
- If you have a buyer's agent/showing assistant this would further decrease your profit.
- This has not even taken into consideration your broker split or if you are a broker this does not include your office overhead.

   To make these examples simple the cost to obtain listings from past clients and sphere of influence is $1000 per month and the third party (Zillow, realtor.com, etc.) costs $800 per month but the ROI is greater to market to your database and past clients.

Well this is great if you have a past client and good sphere of influence in your database. But what if you don't have past clients? Prospecting by phone or door knocking is even cheaper. More time consuming, but cheaper.

This second example is why we focus on Listings for Profit. In both examples we didn't even consider the time it takes to service the buyers. I will say, at some point in your career, you will need to include marketing whether it's a third party source or you market direct via Google, Facebook, magazine, or direct mail. You have to look at all the numbers to determine your profit.

Don't Buy your Way to more Buyers!
Invest in Listings. Buyers will come your way!

Chapter 10
Planting the Seeds

Below is an outline step by step guide to build your listing business.

Day 1 - 3

Build your database in your CRM or on a Spreadsheet. List everybody you know and would like to know. The list should include Full Name, Address, Email, Mobile Phone number, and Birthday. If you have additional information like anniversaries, spouse and kids names and birthdays add this also.

Experienced agents skip to week 3

Week 1 – 2

- **Speak to** (not call) 25 People per day. Start with A and the week with Z
- Send out five handwritten letters daily to sphere of influence, past clients, and/or prospects
- Email or Text 20 people per day with something of value or market updates

Goal - Get 2 listing appointments per week.

Week 3

- Continue everything from week 1-2
- Create your top 50 and Top 20 list. Top 50 are people who you feel are your top 50 contacts that you would like to stay in relationship with and build business with. This could be other business owners, influential friends and associates. Your top 20 lists are your VIP.

- Have coffee, lunch or after work cocktail/snack with 1 person in your VIP once a week
- Contact 1 person per day in your Top 50 with birthday/anniversary/ etc. calls. Out of 50 people today is something to somebody. This is easy to find out with sites like Facebook and Linked in. Someone is celebrating something.
- Keep in mind your top 20 may also be in your top 50, but your top 20 VIP should stand out overall.

Goal 3-4 listing appointments per week

Week 4

Continue and repeat the previous week's activities
Set up tracking system to track the following
1. Number of contacts made
2. Number of letters sent
3. Number of appointments
4. Number of listings taken

If you don't have an income goal for the year, set one. If you have a goal, reset it using the numbers you tracked above and the following system.

If your goal is to earn $150,000 for the year, use the numbers you have from tracking to determine what actions are needed to achieve your goal.

Average sales price $170,000
Multiplied by Average commission $170,000x3% = $5,100
Goal $150,000 divided by commission $5,100 = Closing needed 29.4

You only need 30 closings a year to reach your goal. **But wait there's more!**

Remember I mentioned digging deeper into the numbers for **Profit.** Well this is no different.

Do you want to make $150,000 or Net $150,000 after expenses?

Also in order to close 30 transactions you have to look at other factors

The REAL numbers of Real Estate

1. How many contacts before you got an appointment, how many appointments before you got a listing, and how many listings actually sold.

2. What is your listing to closing ratio? (if you don't have one use your office ratio) This is the percentage of listings that you take that actually close. For this example let's say you close 70% of your listings

Let's say
You have 30 contacts before you schedule 1 appointment.

You have 3 appointments before you when 1 listing

80% of your listings sale

You need 30 closings to reach your goal

You actually need 38 listings 38x80%=30.4

To get 38 listings you need 114 listing appointments
38 listings at a 3 x 1 conversion
3 appointments to get 1 listing.
3 x 38 = 114

To get 114 appointments you need 3420 Contacts
3420 Contacts at a 30 x 1 conversion
30 Contacts to get 1 appointment.
30 x 114 appointments = 3420

3420 contacts to earn $150,000

Now if you answered you want to net $150,000 this changes even more. You have to consider taxes, office expenses and brokerage fees, commission splits, MLS fees, board dues and other expenses.

You may actually need to make $225,000 to $235,000 to net $150,000 depending on your tax filings and previous mentioned expenses. Now you have to change all your action numbers to reflect $235,000 as a goal. So you actually need more closings to net the $150,000.

Goal- 1 Listing appointment per day. 1 Listing Per week

Week 5

Continue and repeat the previous week's activities
Track your numbers and adjust as needed.
Schedule your education and vacation days for the remainder of the year.

The reason you schedule your education in advance is because it stops you from last minute spending on what you think you may need. This also allows you time in between training and classes to apply what you learned to your business.

Scheduling your vacation lets you and your teams know, in advance, when you will be away from your business. You may have to double down on activities 2-3 weeks before vacation and 2-3 weeks after vacation to keep on track for your yearly goals. I like spontaneous trips and vacations but I understand what this can do to business also if done too often. Life emergencies and kids are spontaneous enough.

Leave room on your calendar for adjustments if needed. Adjustments like emergencies will happen. When your action calendar is scheduled you can simply pick back up when you return and take yesterday's action items and double up on activities today.

You either need inventory or you need to have control of the inventory to attract buyers and more sellers.

Remember without inventory in the store why would people shop there.

Zillow and Amazon are both examples of how to control inventory they don't have.

Now you have to figure out a way to have the most listing inventory in your market.

The other option is to figure out a way to control the housing inventory in your market.

Either way you List and you Live

We recommend using our Sowing Seeds for Listing Leads Prospecting Journal to help you track the following activities:

Past Clients/Sphere of Influence - Friends, family, and past buyers who are now potential sellers. Typically they will sell on average of every 7 years.

FSBO - For Sale by Owner

Absentee Owners - Investors and Vacation Home property owners

Probate - Contact the executor/personal representative or attorney for the estate

Expired Listings - Homes listed for sale that did not close

Circle Prospecting Just Listed/Just Sold - Call 100-500 homes surrounding your current listings or just sold listings.

Neighborhood Farm - A target area that you market to on a consistent regular basis. Your goal is the be the agent of choice and first in mind when homeowners in the area think of real estate

Made in the USA
Columbia, SC
06 January 2025